cool collectibles
# DOLLS

Kristine Hooks

HIGH
interest
books

Children's Press
A Division of Grolier Publishing
New York / London / Hong Kong / Sydney
Danbury, Connecticut

*To my mother, Carol Hooks, and my grandmother, Dorothy DePan*

Book Design: Michael DeLisio
Contributing Editor: Jennifer Ceaser

Photo Credits: Cover © Werner H. Müller/Corbis; p. 5, 11, 14, 20, © Indexstock Imagery; p. 6 © Araldo deLuca/Corbis; p. 13 © Peter Harholdt/Corbis; p.16 © Corbis/Reuters; p. 19, 25 © AFP/Corbis; p. 22, 33 © Indexstock Photography; p. 23 © Jacques M. Chenet/ Corbis; p. 27 © UPI/Corbis-Bettman; p. 28 © Laura Dwight/Corbis; p. 31, 40 by Dean Galiano (Britney Spears doll reproduced courtesy of Signatures Network); p. 36 © Reuters/Corbis-Bettman

Visit Children's Press on the Internet at:
http://publishing.grolier.com

Library of Congress Cataloging-in-Publication Data

Hooks, Kristine.
  Dolls / by Kristine Hooks.
    p. cm. – (Cool collectibles)
  Includes bibliographical references and index.
  Summary: Discusses the history of dolls and explains how to start and maintain a doll collection.
  ISBN 0-516-23330-0 (lib. bdg.) – ISBN 0-516-23530-3 (pbk.)
  1. Dolls—Collectors and collecting—Juvenile literature. 2. Dolls—History—Juvenile literature. [1. Dolls—Collectors and collecting. 2. Dolls—History. 3 Collectors and collecting.] I. Title. II. Series.

NK4893.H59 2000
688.7'221'075—dc21

00-027945

# Contents

Introduction 4

1 All About Dolls 7

2 Collecting–What to Look For 17

3 Starting and Keeping a Doll Collection 29

New Words 42

For Further Reading 44

Resources 46

Index 47

About the Author 48

# Introduction

People collect things for many different reasons. Some people enjoy collecting items they really love. Many young collectors enjoy sharing their collections with friends. Some collectors like the challenge of discovering rare items. Others build up a collection to make a profit.

Dolls are one of people's most favorite items to collect. This book will help you learn the basics of doll collecting. You'll find out about the history of dolls and the types of dolls that people collect. You'll discover where to find collectible dolls, what to look for when buying a doll, and how to determine the value (worth) of a doll. You'll also learn how to display your doll collection so that you can share the beauty of your dolls with others.

These antique dolls range from fifty to two hundred years old.

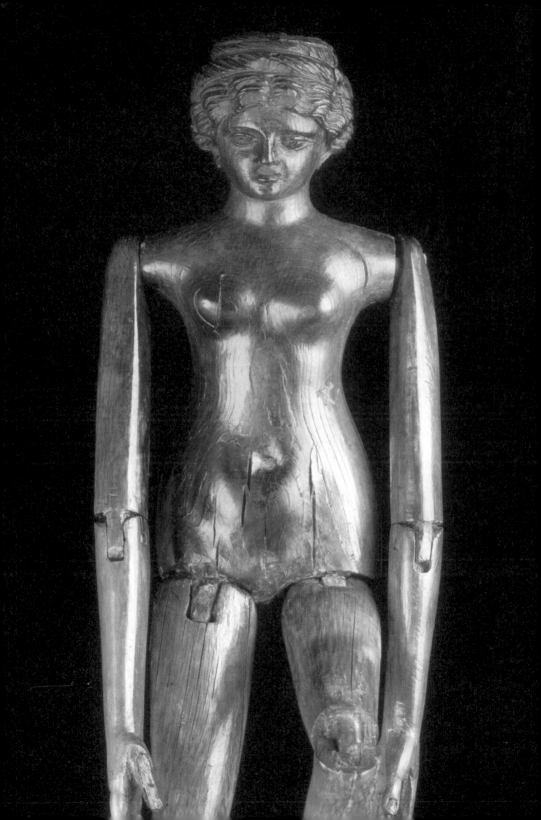

# 1

# All About Dolls

Dolls have been around for thousands of years. They are one of the oldest toys known in the world. Dolls have been a part of almost every culture—from that of the ancient Aztecs to Europe in the Middle Ages to colonial America.

Some of the oldest dolls were rag dolls made from simple, stuffed fabrics. Other dolls were carved from wood. Dolls' features, such as eyes and hair, were made using pieces of clay, wood beads, or fabric. In the 1800s, dolls started being constructed from porcelain or bisque (china). Their features were hand painted. Often, real human hair decorated the dolls' heads. In the 1900s, papier-mâché (paper mixed with glue, clay, or flour) and wax dolls

Dolls are one of the oldest known toys in the world.

became very popular. With the invention of vinyl and plastic in the twentieth century, dolls were produced much more quickly and cheaply.

It wasn't until the 1970s that doll collecting became an international hobby and an enormous business. Value guides (which report the selling prices of dolls) were introduced. Doll picture books and national doll magazines were published. Doll shows (fairs) became popular. People started to see doll collecting as an investment rather than as just a simple hobby.

**FUN FACT**

Dolls have been found buried with people who lived more than four thousand years ago!

## TYPES OF DOLLS

Dolls come in all shapes and sizes. There are dozens of different types of dolls that a person can collect. Sometimes a doll is characterized by the type of material from which it is made.

Examples of materials from which dolls are made include:

- bisque (unglazed porcelain, usually with a pink tint)
- china (same as porcelain)
- cloth
- composition (a mixture of many materials including sawdust, small pieces of wood, glue, and flour)
- kid body (body of white or pink leather)
- papier-mâché
- parian (very fine type of white porcelain)
- plastic
- porcelain (glazed ceramic)
- wax
- wax over (made of papier-mâché or composition and covered with a layer of wax)
- wood
- vinyl (soft plastic material)

A doll may be characterized by the category it falls into or its brand name. Some examples of these categories or brands are:

- American Girl™

- artist (created by well-known doll artists)

- baby doll

- bébé (type of French china doll)

- Barbie®

- boudoir (original dolls in very fancy, often hand-sewn, clothes)

- ethnic (dolls of various races)

- Frozen Charlotte (dolls molded all in one piece; arms and legs don't move)

- Ginny®

- international (dolls clothed in foreign costume)

- Kewpie

- Madame Alexander™

- vintage (old dolls)

A person who collects dolls could have a very general collection—any kind of doll that he or she likes could be in the collection. Or, a person could focus on a specific type of doll.

For example, you might collect only porcelain dolls, but your collection could include porcelain dolls from all the companies that have ever made these dolls. A very specialized collector will focus on one particular kind of

This collection focuses just on Raggedy Ann and Andy items.

doll. This person may have a collection of just Raggedy Ann and Raggedy Andy dolls, or a collection of bisque dolls made in France between 1880 and 1900. If you collect only Barbie dolls or only American Girl dolls, it means that you are specializing in that type of doll.

11

## DOLL CHARACTERISTICS

As you learn more about dolls, there are certain features you will begin to notice. These features help you to understand more about the type of doll.

- **Hair** Is the hair painted on? Is it molded hair (curls or waves that are part of the actual mold)? Or is the hair a wig? Wigs can be made from animal, synthetic (man-made), or human hair. The hair might be sewn into or glued onto the head.

- **Head and Neck** From what type of material is the head made? (On older dolls, the head is porcelain, and the body is made of cloth.) Are the head, neck, and shoulders all one piece (a shoulder head)? Or do the head and neck fit into a hole in the shoulder area (a socket head)?

- **Eyes** Are the eyes fixed (do not move or close), flirting (moving from side to side), sleeping (weights or wires make the eyes close) or googly (large, round eyes that look to one side)?

These bisque dolls have wigs of human hair attached to their heads.

- **Body Parts** Are the body parts fixed in one position or can you move them? Do the parts have joints? From what materials are the body parts made?

## IS IT A COLLECTIBLE?

Not all kinds of dolls are considered to be good collectibles. Serious doll collectors look for dolls that are very valuable. A doll is considered valuable for the following reasons:

- it is very old (but in good condition)
- it is very rare
- it was/is of very high quality

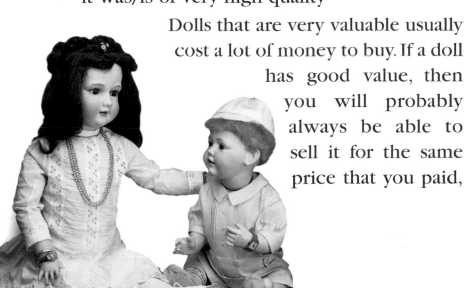

Dolls that are very valuable usually cost a lot of money to buy. If a doll has good value, then you will probably always be able to sell it for the same price that you paid,

13

or maybe even more. The average price for buying or selling a certain kind of collectible doll can be found in a book called a value guide. Value guides are available at bookstores and hobby shops.

It is very important to remember that just because something does not have good value as a collectible, this does not mean that you should not collect it. If you love little plastic dolls that you get out of a gumball machine, you should collect those. You may not ever be able to sell them for a lot of money, but they still are valuable to you! In fact, even the most serious doll collector doesn't buy a doll just for the money that can be made from it. Most doll collectors cherish all the dolls in their collection, no matter how much they are worth.

**FUN FACT**

The most valuable Barbie doll is a 1959 model, which is valued at more than $5,000.

These tiny, antique dolls are wonderful items to collect.

# 2

# Collecting—What to Look For

Kammer & Reinhardt was one of the companies making German bisque children dolls in the early 1900s. If you wanted to buy Kammer & Reinhardt's Model No. 105 today, you would have to pay about $170,000. Model No. 106 would sell for almost $145,000. Many people can buy a house for less than the cost of these dolls!

Does this mean that you have to be rich to be a doll collector? Absolutely not! As you have read, the most important thing to remember about collecting is that you should collect a doll because it appeals to you. There are many different kinds of dolls that sell for closer to $17 than $170,000.

You don't have to spend a lot of money on dolls to start a collection.

## AFFORDABLE DOLLS

Doll collectors who do not have a lot of money to invest should begin by looking for dolls for sale in most toy stores. Most of these dolls are mass-produced, which means that a large number of them were manufactured. In general, the more available a doll is to the public, the less value it has. Therefore, a doll with less value usually will not cost a lot of money to purchase. For example, the average Barbie doll sells in a toy store for about $10.

Modern doll manufacturers make all types of dolls. Some companies, such as the Madame Alexander company, make dolls that are meant to be keepsakes (collectibles). Other kinds of modern dolls, including fashion dolls (Barbie and other dress-up dolls), celebrity dolls (Spice Girls, Britney Spears), and movie character dolls (from *Star Wars*), are good for young doll collectors. With so many different types of dolls to choose from, you will definitely find something

Barbie dolls are some of the most affordable dolls to collect.

When buying an antique doll, make sure that it's in good condition.

to collect that fits in your budget and matches your personal style!

## JUDGING A DOLL'S VALUE

It has been said that you should always collect from the heart. If you make some money later, that is just an added bonus. Of course, that does not mean you should not pay any attention to money. You do have to buy the dolls for your collection, after all. So, how do you know whether the doll you want is worth the money? To be a good judge of value, you should be familiar with important collecting guidelines.

## Marks

Does the doll have a marking or a label that tells who made the doll and when it was made? A marked doll allows you to be sure of what you are buying. Marks and labels identify one or more of the following about a doll:

- manufacturer
- trade name of the doll
- country where the doll was made
- style or mold number
- date the doll was made

These marks or labels can be found stamped on the doll's body (usually on the bottoms of the feet, the back, or the back of the head). Labels also may be sewn onto the doll's clothing.

## Quality

Is the doll well made and of high quality? The quality of the work done on dolls can vary, even if they come from the same mold. Are the doll's features well painted? Is the doll's expression believable? You will be able to judge quality after you have learned more about different types of dolls. With experience, you will be able to com-pare the quality of one dollmaker's work to another dollmaker's work.

This high-quality Mardis Gras doll has well-painted features.

## Condition

Is the doll in good condition? Are there large cracks or several chips in the porcelain? Is the doll missing body parts, such as fingers? Are painted features fading or are they still bright? Are all of the clothes and accessories included and in good condition? Are all the parts of the doll original? How much of the doll has been restored (fixed up or replaced with newer parts)?

If a doll is in mint condition, it means that it is in perfect condition. This is especially true if the doll is still in its original clothing, and the clothing is in good condition. Often the best way to have a mint condition doll is to keep it in its original packaging.

This Cabbage Patch doll from the 1980s still has its original clothing.

## Age and Size

An old doll is not necessarily worth more than a newer doll. Some Barbies from the 1960s are worth more than German bisque dolls of the 1890s. However, a doll's size does affect its value. In general, the larger the doll, the higher its price and the greater its value.

## Popularity and Availability

If a particular doll was once very popular, there may be many people who want to have the doll for sentimental reasons. One example of this type of popular doll is Chatty Cathy, a doll that was made in the 1960s. People who grew up when Chatty Cathy dolls were popular like to collect these dolls. They may enjoy being reminded of when they were younger.

However, because Chatty Cathy dolls are no longer made, there are not enough of them available to collectors. This shortage of dolls means that there is an availability problem. The less available a certain doll is, the more rare it is. A doll's rarity can drive up the demand for the doll and raise its value.

The 40th Anniversary Barbie doll, decorated with real diamonds, had limited availability.

There also can be an availability problem for newly manufactured dolls. This is often true when a doll is a limited edition. Limited edition means that only a limited (specific) number were made. Even mass-produced dolls, such as Barbie, will occasionally come out with a special limited edition. Recently, the 40th Anniversary Gala Barbie was produced, but it was only available to members of the Official Barbie Collector's Club.

## Visual Appeal

Another factor that affects the price and value of a doll is its visual appeal. Visual appeal is very hard to measure. It's easy to tell whether a doll is well made or in good condition. It's much harder to judge whether the doll is so attractive or stylish that it will be valuable. What is appealing today may not be tomorrow. You will have to decide whether the doll's beauty makes it worth the cost.

## REPRODUCTIONS AND RESTORATION

If you really want to add that $170,000 doll to your collection but cannot afford it, consider these two options:

- Look for modern reproductions (copies) of the antique doll that you have been admiring. You may find reproductions by searching the Internet or looking through doll collecting magazines. A reproduction is not as valuable as an original, but it doesn't cost as much, either!

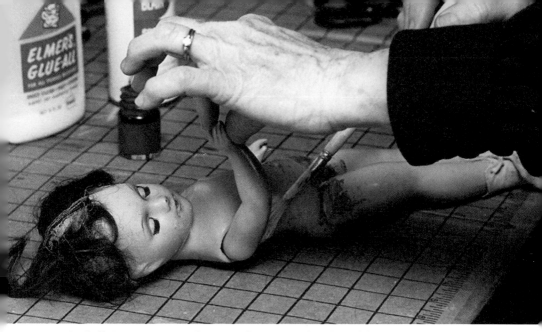

A doll in poor condition often can be fixed by an expert in doll restoration.

- Look for a doll that is in poor condition and try to restore it to its former glory. A restored doll has more value than does a reproduction, but less value than an original that is in excellent condition. You can learn some basic restoration techniques by consulting books, such as *The Handbook of Doll Repair and Restoration* by Marty Westfall. You also can locate professional doll restorers by looking in the telephone book under Dolls–Repairing. Be sure to get an estimate before you have any restoration work done.

# 3

# Starting and Keeping a Doll Collection

Are you ready to start collecting dolls? Here are some ways to make your doll collection the best it can be.

## DEFINE YOUR COLLECTION

The main thing to remember when starting your collection is to collect what you like. However, because there are so many different kinds of dolls, it may help to define your collection. Figure out whether you want to concentrate on a certain type of doll or brand of doll. Maybe you just want to collect Barbie dolls. Or perhaps you want a collection of dolls with outfits from foreign countries. The possibilities for building a unique collection are endless. However, if you don't define your collection,

You can start a doll collection with any dolls you like.

you might end up with a random assortment of dolls. (Of course, this is fine, if a random collection is what you want.)

## EDUCATE YOURSELF

Learn as much as you can about the type of dolls that you want to collect. Read doll magazines and check out doll Web sites. Learn what features to look for in your type of doll. Find out what the average price of a doll in your collection costs. Check out value guides to see the prices at which dolls are selling. Go to doll shows to see the prices and conditions of dolls. The more you know, the easier it will be for you to decide on the type of doll that you want to collect. Your research also will help you figure out whether that doll type is in your budget.

## CREATE A BUDGET

It's easy to get carried away when you start a doll collection. So, it's important to decide how much you can spend each week or month on

Doll clothing and props should be included in your budget.

dolls. Decide whether you want to save up for one big doll purchase or whether you want to buy a less expensive doll each month or so. Remember to include accessories, such as clothing or props, in your budget.

## GO SHOPPING!

The final (and most fun) thing to do is shop for dolls. You know the type of doll for which you are looking. You also have determined how much you can spend. So, where do you go to buy your dolls?

## Stores

Dolls can be bought in toy stores both large and small. They can be found in the toy section of department and chain stores, such as WalMart. You also may be able to find dolls in special hobby shops. Check your local Yellow Pages for listings under Hobby or Dolls.

## Garage Sales, Craft Shows, and Flea Markets

Check your local newspaper for garage sales or yard sales. You may get lucky and find a great doll at a very inexpensive price.

Look for advertisements in the newspaper for craft shows, at which unique, handmade dolls may be sold. Check your local phone directory for permanent flea markets in your area. There is often a lot of junk sold at flea markets, but you may come across a real find!

Among all the junk, you may spot a doll you like at a
garage sale or flea market.

## Advertisements

In most doll collecting magazines, there are
advertisements for companies selling dolls
through the mail. You can buy either new dolls or
antique dolls. To order from these companies, you
have to send a check or money order in the mail.

You also can order over the phone with a
credit card. There is no guarantee in what

33

condition the dolls will be. Some collectors may only want to buy a doll if they can see it first.

If you buy a doll through the mail, be sure the company is sending you the doll you want. Check to see that the doll is in the same condition in which it was advertised. If it is not, call the company and ask for your money back.

## A Family Affair

Tell family members about your interest in doll collecting. Doll collecting may be an activity all of you can enjoy together. You also may need your family's help and support to become a doll collector. For example, you may need someone to drive you to local doll shops, flea markets, and doll shows.

Also, if you want to shop at online auctions, you may need to ask someone with a credit card or a checking account to pay for your transaction.

## Doll Shows

Check your local newspaper for doll shows coming to your area. Visiting these shows can be fun whether or not you buy any dolls. You will get to see a wide selection of dolls from both past and present. Doll shows also are a good way to meet people who have a similar interest. You also will be able to see a doll and check out its condition before you buy it.

## Internet

You might be able to find the doll you want at an online auction. An auction is a public sale in which items are sold to people who make the highest bids. A bid is when you say how much you will pay for something.

If you have an Internet connection, you can go to an auction Web site, such as Amazon.com or eBay. If you find a doll you like, you can place a bid, which is the highest amount of money you are willing to spend on the doll. If someone

else places a higher bid, you can raise your bid, or you can let the other bidder buy the doll.

Many people enjoy the fun of placing bids, but you should always be careful not to bid more than you can really spend. Remember, if you win a doll at an auction, you still have to pay money for it. You will have to send a check or money order in the mail to the seller. Then the seller sends you the doll you bought at the auction.

## MAINTAIN YOUR COLLECTION

It's important to maintain your dolls so that they stay in the best possible condition. Your collection of modern Barbies may be valuable someday, but not if the dolls are in poor shape.

Maintaining your collection doesn't mean that you can't play with the dolls. Of course, some collectors prefer dolls that are in their original packaging. For this reason, collectors who want to pose or play with their dolls will buy two versions of each doll. One doll is saved

This collector poses with just a few of the seven hundred Barbie dolls in her collection.

in its original package and the other is for handling. Buying two of the same doll is not necessary if you follow some important rules:

- Play carefully with your dolls. Handle them gently. Do not change your dolls by brushing hair, removing items that are permanently attached, or making marks of any kind.

- Keep good records. If you take a doll out of its original package, write down the name of the doll, the manufacturer, the year it was made, where you bought it, and how much you paid. Also, if you are going to mix and match clothes and accessories, keep a list of which ones came with each doll.

- If something happens to a doll, try to fix it as soon as possible. However, never clean or repair a doll if you aren't sure what will happen. Most modern dolls can be cleaned with soap and water. This type of cleaning may not be appropriate for more fragile dolls.

# DISPLAY YOUR COLLECTION

Now that you've bought your dolls, don't forget to display them! Displaying your dolls is a fun way to show off your collection. Set aside some shelves in your bookshelf or find a nice display case with glass windows. Make sure that the shelves are safe from damage by pets or children. Also, try to keep your dolls away from dust and sunlight—both of which can slowly destroy the dolls.

## FUN FACT

Some very famous celebrities collect dolls. When Barbie celebrated her fortieth birthday with parties around the world, stars such as Melissa Joan Hart and Drew Carey attended the popular celebrations.

Olympic superstar Jackie Joyner-Kersee loves Barbie and Barbie accessories—she has a huge collection of more than five hundred Barbie dolls!

## ENJOY COLLECTING

You have to think about a lot of different things when you become a doll collector. If it seems confusing at first, don't get frustrated. You will learn more and more as you read doll collecting magazines, look at value guides, and visit doll shops and doll shows. Don't be afraid to ask questions! A good way to get answers to doll-related questions is to join a doll collector's chat group on the Internet or a doll collecting club in your town. In this way, you can share the joy of doll collecting with other doll lovers. And most important, always remember to collect for love, not money!

The Britney Spears doll was "Born To Make You Happy."

# New Words

**artist doll**  doll created by a well-known doll artist

**auction**  a public sale in which things are sold to people who make the highest bids

**bébé**  a type of French china doll

**bisque**  unglazed porcelain, usually with a pink tint

**boudoir doll**  original, very elaborately clothed doll

**china**  see definition at porcelain

**collection**  an assortment of items that are collected for interest

**composition**  mixture of many materials, including sawdust, small pieces of wood, glue, and flour

**ethnic dolls**  dolls of various races

**fixed eyes**  eyes that do not move or close

**flirting eyes**  eyes that move from side to side

**Frozen Charlotte**  doll molded all in one piece; arms and legs don't move

**glazed**  given a shiny finish

**googly eyes**  large, round eyes that look to one side

**international doll**  doll clothed in a foreign costume

**investment**  something on which money is spent

**kid body**  body of white or pink leather

**mint condition**  perfect condition

**mold**  used to create the shape of an object

**molded hair**  curls and waves that look like hair and that are part of the actual mold

**papier-mâché**  paper mixed with glue, clay, or flour

**parian**  very fine type of white porcelain

**porcelain**  glazed ceramic

**rare**  difficult to find

**reproduction**  copy

**restore**  fix up

**sleeping eyes**  eyes that close by means of weights or wires

**value guide**  book that gives the selling prices of dolls

**vinyl**  soft plastic material

**visual appeal**  the beauty or style of a doll

**wax over**  doll made of papier-mâché or composition and covered with a layer of wax

# For Further Reading

## Books

Foulke, Jan. *14th Blue Book: Dolls and Values.* Grantsville, MD: Hobby House Press, 1999.

Mandeville, A. Glenn, Marl Davidson, Priscilla Wardlow and Gary R. Ruddell. *Barbie® Doll Collector's Handbook.* Grantsville, MD: Hobby House Press, 1997.

Manolis, Argie, ed. *The Doll Sourcebook.* Cincinnati, OH: F & W Publishing, Inc., 1996.

Rozakis, Laurie E. *The Complete Idiot's Guide to Buying and Selling Collectibles.* Old Tappan, NJ: Macmillan Publishing Company, 1997.

Westfall, Marty. *The Handbook of Doll Repair and Restoration.* New York: Crown Publishing, 1997.

## Magazines

*Doll Reader*
6405 Flank Drive
Harrisburg, PA 17112
800-829-3340

*Dolls*
170 Fifth Avenue, 12th Floor
New York, NY 10010
800-588-1691

# Resources

**Barbie.com**

*www.barbie.com*

The official Barbie Web site includes the history of the Barbie doll and doll value information.

**Doll Collecting**

*www.collectdolls.about.com*

A site that includes articles and resources about dolls and doll collecting. It includes doll reviews and links to other sites about dolls.

**iDolls.com—The Ultimate Doll Resource**

*www.iDolls.com*

This site features an online doll store and auction site that lets you design your own doll. It also provides information about new doll products.

# Index

**A**

accessories, 31, 38
American Girl™, 10, 11
artist doll, 10
auction, 35, 37

**B**

baby doll, 10
Barbie ®, 10, 11, 15, 18, 23, 25,
    29, 37, 39
bébé doll, 10
bisque, 7, 9, 11, 17, 24
body parts, 13, 22
boudoir doll, 10

**C**

celebrity dolls, 18
Chatty Cathy, 24
china (see also porcelain), 7, 9
composition, 9
condition, 13, 22, 23, 26, 27,
    34, 37
craft shows, 32

**D**

display your collection, 39

doll characteristics, 12, 13
doll shows, 8, 30, 35, 41

**E**

ethnic dolls, 10

**F**

fixed eyes, 12
flea markets, 32
flirting eyes, 12
Frozen Charlotte, 10

**G**

garage sales, 32
Ginny®, 10
googly eyes, 12

**I**

international doll, 10

**J**

judging a doll's value, 20–26

**K**

Kammer & Reinhardt, 17
keepsakes, 18
Kewpie, 10
kid body, 9

# Index

**L**
limited edition, 25

**M**
Madame Alexander™, 10, 18
marks, 21
mint condition, 23
mold, 22
molded hair, 12
movie character dolls, 18

**P**
pâpier-maché, 7, 9
parian, 9
porcelain, 7, 9, 11, 12, 22

**Q**
quality, 22

**R**
Raggedy Ann and Andy, 11

rare, 4, 13, 24
reproduction(s), 26, 27
restoration, 26, 27

**S**
shoulder head, 12
sleeping eyes, 12
socket head, 12

**V**
value guide(s), 8, 15, 30, 41
vintage doll, 10
vinyl, 8, 9
visual appeal, 26

**W**
wax over, 9
where to find dolls, 32–37

## ABOUT THE AUTHOR

Kristine Hooks is a lawyer living in New York City. She keeps a small collection of old dolls that she acquired from her grandmother. Kristine also remembers the dolls of her childhood, including Barbie and Chrissy, with great fondness.